Subterranean
Red

Subterranean Red

Kathleen Johnson

MONGREL EMPIRE PRESS
NORMAN, OKLAHOMA, UNITED STATES OF AMERICA

Norman, Oklahoma
2012

FIRST EDITION, 2012

Subterranean Red © 2012
by Kathleen Johnson

ISBN 978-0-9833052-7-9

Cover Image: *Family Tree* by Soleil Johnson.
Used by permission.

MONGREL EMPIRE PRESS
NORMAN, OK

ONLINE CATALOGUE: WWW.MONGRELEMPIRE.ORG

This publisher is a proud member of

$[\textbf{clmp}]$

COUNCIL OF LITERARY MAGAZINES & PRESSES
W W W . C L M P . O R G

For Scott

What will we become?
Cool shadows in the red
mineral belly of the earth?

—Anita Endrezze,
"The Language of Fossils"

Contents

Mixed-Blood Memories

Cimarron Breaks

Notes on Illustrations

Mixed-Blood Memories

Cherokee blood, if not destroyed, will win its courses in beings of fair complexions, who will read that their ancestors became civilized under the frowns of misfortunes, and the causes of their enemies.

—John Ridge, born Skah-tle-loh-skee
(Yellow Bird), 1802-1839

No amount of white blood shall dilute the pride of the Cherokee people—nor erase their memories.

—Cherokee Chief Charles Renatus Hicks,
1767-1827

The Apothecary of Minerva Best

My world fell away long ago.

I'm left with an ache as faint
and elusive as the sound in
a conch put to my ear.
The ebb and flow now
no more than a murmur
or a memory.
Sometimes I try
to recall the embraces,
even a lover's phrases, now faded
as red ochre paintings
etched on the walls of a cave,
drawn and abandoned.

I no longer wish or want.
I occupy the earth
in the still space of a stone.

But at night my dreams try
to take me home; I struggle in a fever
to find my way back to
where I've never been.
I search highways, hidden places,
memories, names, faces. I tunnel
through mountains and dark passages
under the stark face of the moon.

I know home.
It is as a red place. I remember
and imagine a red place.
I can almost see
my loved ones there.

So I find solace in sunsets,
dying embers of a fire,
the mud beneath my feet.

I make medicine under the proper moon,
gather plants in wild places
no one else knows.
With each passing season,
my knowledge of the old ways grows.

My kitchen shelves are lined with remedies—
jars and baskets full of roots, leaves, and berries.
There's willow bark to ease pain,
wild geranium to stop bleeding,
sweet violet to calm nerves.

My kitchen window's amber square of light
comforts those who pass by at night.

Though I live restless and alone
at the edge of the woods,
the deer who come to drink
from the stream keep me company.
When I look into that moonlit water,
faces surface,
faces without features.

I search my own dark eyes
in the mirror, looking for
the road home.
I take wrong turns.
Along the way,
I recognize the rattlesnake,
the owl, coyotes running under stars.
My mind is a sky clouded with stories,

but when I open my eyes in the dark,
I find them moving fast away.

These are my prayers:
sunflower and corn pollen,
hickory wood, sumac bark.

Yet, in the evening sky, a pair of ravens
can suddenly break my heart.

I have become a woman
of spare charms and few words.

I can't find my way here.
I can't find my way home.
I'm lost
in some ragged country
between birth and death
and I'm being led on a trail.

Three Generations of Cherokee Women: A Portrait

In the photo it is 1962, when I was three,
and here are three of us:
Great-grandmother, Mother, me.
Pearl, the eldest, looks straight
into the camera. Mother to eight,
born in Indian Territory in 1887,
she's seen them come and seen them
go. The stories she could tell
I'll never know. But her hands look like
they've wrung a thousand chicken necks;
she wears a rhinestone brooch.
Her graying hair is pulled back in a bun,
the way she's worn it since she was a girl.
Despite the winter glare, her gaze holds
steady, sure. My mother, as always, tries
to look pretty—and succeeds, as always,
though squinting into Oklahoma sun.
She touches my shoulder, the lace
of my red velvet dress, with one
tentative finger, as if she could keep
me there in her slight grasp
forever. I look to the shadows.

Spring Pilgrimage to Tahlequah

On the road to visiting the land of ancestors I don't remember
I pass the land of ancestors I do remember, the highway
a snake slithering through past lives, slithering across
a rugged country of red buttes and mesas. Family
lies surround me still, echo off steep cliffs of
the Cimarron, hang thick in the humid
Oklahoma air.   Funnel cloud or
ghost rider in the sky carrying
secrets?   I listen hard for
stories never told.
All I hear is
thunder.

Wild Sand Plums

Picking time again.
Another scorching summer
in Oklahoma, horseflies circling close
around my ears, sleepy clouds above
in sky June-blue as prairie flax.

I pick from the riverbank bushes
with care, the way Mother did,
watching for rattlers or a copperhead,
seeking out plums the deepest red,
those dead ripe and sweet.

My bucket swings heavy with fruit
as I walk the dirt road home,
imagining plump pies,
ruby jars of jelly I'll store
in the root cellar till Christmas.

I pass by the empty house
where Mother lived when she was a girl.
She's gone a year now. Her heart gave out
here in the same county she was born into,
barely a mile from the old homeplace.

Meadowlarks and scissortails line
phone wires. Their calls
only I can hear—no one else about
forever. I join in with a tune
Grandmother would sing when we walked
together, the only words I ever heard
in the old language, a song her mother sang
on the forced march from Georgia.

The day before she died,
I heard my mother singing
that song in English:

Guide me, oh Jehovah, on this path
here below. You are very strong,
and I am very weak.
All the time, all the time,
help me, all the time.

Roadside sunflowers face the sun,
sway in the wind.
Near the cornfield, I bend
to pick up a mottled feather.

Grandmothers, Mother, me.
On this path here below,
we walk together.

Ghost

She has been drained of color
until invisible. Nobody
looks at her now.
She sees her life
behind her: a cold landscape
shot through with red.
There were the days before,
the days after.
Snow dusts the ground,
covers it like a gauzy shroud.
Who can wake this world?
A bear growls unheard
in the distance.
Ravens wheel in forbidding skies,
dark as her dreams.
She waits for a saving voice.
She hears only her own
wretched, beautiful, lusty wail.

In Wildwood Cemetery
Sarah Childers Shamblin 1812-1857

You might be wearing
your best dress—crimson calico—
as you lie in the cold clay

of Wildwood Cemetery.
North Georgia oaks grow tall
around your grave.

A full Trading Moon
shines down Childress Hollow Road,
whitens your headstone,

glows red
as hearth coals as it sinks
behind Lookout Mountain.

Two hundred years after your birth,
I've spent months trying to unearth
deep Cherokee roots, trying to find

you, mysterious ancestor.
Who were your parents?
What happened to your eight children?

This I know: after you died,
your husband, Archibald, married
another Cherokee woman,

the widow Meadow. He lived
thirty years more, lies buried
next to you. I want to know who

you were, what of you lives on
in me—in my daughter—
why I feel I know you,

though I know only your name
and the tangled woods where you remain.
Blood is blood, Sarah. Let's trade

secrets; tonight we share
the same November moonlight,
but we're both still in the dark.

Cherokee Grandfather
A.S. Watson 1906-1974

He played checkers and dominoes with us, dubbed my
brother and cousin Poncho and Cisco, teased me about
riding in the rumble seat of a little red roadster, went with
us to the pond in the boondocks to fish, took us to play
on the old tar-black train at the park, let us try out the
typewriter and telegraph in the Santa Fe depot where he
worked, taught us to eat watermelon in the backyard, spit
out the seeds, let the juice drip down our chins. These
things I want my children to know. I could play the tape
for them, the cassette I made with the recorder I got for
Christmas in Tulsa in third grade. They could hear his
voice as he recites Poe's "The Raven" and "Annabelle Lee"
and Longfellow's "The Children's Hour" while forgetting
to put his false teeth in. I could tell them that he built a
tree house in the apple tree for us, that he hopped trains
with hobos all the way to California when he looked for
work during the Depression. I could explain that he was
a Sunday-school teacher and Baptist-church deacon, a
railroad man who moved his family from small town to
small town in Oklahoma and Kansas, never took a day of
vacation, and died of a heart attack a few months after he
retired. I wish they could hear the stories he told about
seeing Geronimo, who was an old man, when he was a
child in Indian Territory. I want my children to know
him, though they can't. I want to say he was the fun
grandfather, the one with the twinkling eyes. But that
makes him sound like a Disney character, and he was
anything but that. He lived a life harder than I or they
can imagine. So I will tell them this: His eyes twinkled
the way stars in the Western sky twinkle—like a miracle
in all that darkness.

14

Autobiography in Red

> every red thing in the world
> is the reflection of blood,
> our death and our rising.

> Wendy Rose, "Itch Like Crazy: Resistance"

For your many angles I have many shades. Terra-cotta
hills, rust-colored canyons. Desire advancing, retreating,
nearing, disappearing. All the words painted lips never
say. Cabernet, chrysanthemums, muted ends of endless
days. I'm the witch, the wolf, more crimson truth than
white lie. Know this, my nightmare, *mein Albtraum*:
I wake up burning but alive. I'm outside light sensed
through walls of the womb. Pulse beats that stop when
you enter a room. The sanguine river of language you
swim in. Love's vital script. Death's vitriolic script.
Summer fields of sun-drenched flowers. What catches
the eye and what holds it. Any heart's saturation point.
The scarlet lace I don't wear but admire. The beginning
in blood. The end in fire. I'm Permian beds, satin spar,
Thursday's child who must go far. I rise from dirt, swing
from branches of the family tree (I am they and they are
me). I'm a red-letter day, a red-faced lie, screaming sirens
passing by. I'm why tonight's rhythm hates tomorrow's
rhyme, an Oklahoma cyclone spinning by. I must stop
making sense, let things fall where they may. When all
the dust settles, I'm this bloody battleground I fight with
myself on every day.

Raven Mocker

—from the Cherokee legend

heart stealer
secret keeper
unholy bird
mocker of spirits and witches

secret keeper
rising from a mountain cleft
mocker of spirits and witches
his call in the cold distance

rising from a mountain cleft
corpse   corpse
his call in the cold distance
iridescent as raven feathers his blue-black hair

corpse   corpse
night on his back
iridescent as raven feathers his blue-black hair
broad wings slicing the air

night on his back
he flies in through the window to hasten the dying
broad wings slicing the air
harbinger of fear and final dark

he flies in through the window to hasten the dying
he tortures and torments
harbinger of fear and final dark
red eyes hungry

he tortures and torments
for the taste of a heart
red eyes hungry
grieving kin feel a gust of wind

for the taste of a heart
the rustling flap and whir
grieving kin feel a gust of wind
the gathering of another life into his own

the rustling flap and whir
he flies away trailing sparks like a comet
the gathering of another life into his own
death smell heavy as a curtain around the bed

he flies away trailing sparks like a comet
no heart left in the body
death smell heavy as a curtain around the bed
silhouetted by the silver moon

no heart left in the body
raven mocker preens on the highest bough
silhouetted by the silver moon
heart stealer

Cimarron Breaks

In the bloodline drawn by landscape, all bones are ancestral.

—Teresa Jordan, "Bones"

Ten Seconds after the Gun

A sudden booming of hoof beats
on bone-dry ground.
In the famous Prettyman photo
shot just past noon,
September 16, 1893,
choking dust flies, kicked up by settlers
with Eden in their eyes.
Hell-bent for Oklahoma Territory,
one-hundred-thousand rush the border
in buggies, prairie schooners,
surreys, ox carts,
on nags, mules, race horses.
The camera stills
a fury of horse flesh and heat,
wild-hearted hope,
straw hats, sunbonnets, and Stetsons,
pioneers strewn across
the Cherokee Outlet,
eager to scratch the soil,
for the red-dirt towns to sprout:
Fairview, Buffalo, Freedom, Lookout.

Dust Bowl Diary, 1935

Silt on the dishes.
Rags under the doors.
Horizon coppered by clouds of dirt.
The sun, a dim smear.
No stars, no moon for weeks.
No shadows.

Our farm is sifting away—
only a bit of cornfield stubble
poking up through shifting dunes,
cedars chalked with fine dust,
half-buried fence posts.

Cattle are dying,
their lungs caked with mud.
Others, blinded by blowing grit,
stumble in brown blizzards.

Once my hair shone like corn silk
under the sun. Now it's dull, dry,
wrapped tight in a bun.

After a while, everything
seems the color of vermin,
the color of moths—
dirty wash pinned to
the clothesline,
damp dishcloths
stretched along windowsills.

This spring, no lilacs;
no luster left in Mother's eyes.

I've forgotten the true
colors of things. Even the sky
turns eerie shades I've never seen.

Tonight, before sleep,
I'll lie still
on dusty sheets,
close my swollen eyelids,
and pray for vivid dreams.

Frontier Bride

First year of marriage
in a one-room cabin on the prairie,
and for weeks on end it blows—
whirring at the windowsills,
rattling the walls, bending the creek willows,
billowing my skirts. Endless
gusts of wind I hear with each whipstitch,
with every broom sweep,
constant as my own
breath, whimpering around
the doors of my dreams until I want
to slam them shut. Only
sometimes, late at night
with him, a blessed hush,
when—wedding quilt slipped to the floor,
head thrown back, hair a silky tangle,
orange sickle of moon curving
through the window—
I'm lost
in love wild
as an autumn field.

To the Pilgrim Bard, in Gratitude

In honor of my great-great-grandfather,
the poet Orange Scott Cummins (1846-1928)

I often see you wandering past buffalo wallows, across
black-willow swales, camped under cottonwoods

on creek banks, your mule cart full of bleached bison bones,
the air alive with whippoorwill calls, the ticking whir

of rattlesnakes, wings of wild turkeys rustling in river thickets.
I imagine you writing verse on stripped tree bark, crystallized

gypsum, and flat stones by fitful campfire light. In canyons,
on hilltops, or huddled in your dugout as an Oklahoma

blizzard howls over, you grip pen and paper with weathered
hands under the pale wavering of a kerosene lamp. In 1871,

the Civil War still rattling in your ears, a photographer's
magnesium flare caught that westward slant in your eyes,

wide hat-brim circling above long, scout-style curls. Still,
your writing captured more. Poems about ghosts,

buffalo herds, Indians, cowboys, Scots-Irish ancestors,
and sodbusters lie buried deep in your descendants, colorful

as the buttes and mesas of the Red Hills where you settled
at last. Fires, floods, family feuds—so much gets lost.

But because we have your words, the wonder holds.
Nothing, not even prairie cyclones, can whisk it all away.

Snapshots from Warr Acres

Warr Acres, a suburb of Oklahoma City, 1960-1962

1

See the neatly-mowed front yard into which my mother
dragged his smoldering mattress when my brother set his
bed on fire while I slept in my crib in the room we shared.
Kneeling on the hard floor, freckle-faced Scottie at five,
flicking our father's lighter again and again at the bottom
fringe of his red chenille bedspread.

2

This is the chainlinked backyard I left from when I ran
away with Babesy, the Apache boy next door, when I
was two. Several hours after the police were called, some
neighbors found us. I was clutching a rabbit's tail.

3

Look at these three, sun-washed and bathing-suited,
posing on beach towels in the backyard: me at three,
the pudgy middle-aged woman named Margie who
sometimes babysat me, and my slim and smiling mother,
also named Margie, who was sure that if she were just
pretty enough, or wore enough Shalimar, my father would
stop hiding gift-wrapped bottles of My Sin for other
women in the trunk of his car.

4

Here's the sidewalk in front of my house where my
best friend, Pammy, and I, when we were three, started
walking for blocks along East 56th Street, cars flying past.
We had a nickel. We were going to the store to buy
perfume.

5

And there's the blue Ford in the driveway, me sitting on
my father's lap in the front seat as he drove, both of our
hands on the wheel, vodka still hot on his breath.

6

And no photograph of this, either: my first memory—
of me standing up in my crib next to an open window,
face pressed to the screen, violet evening light in the
west, backyard swingset chains creaking in the breeze.
Me, mute and kneegreen in May, witness to the wholly
untroubled Oklahoma sky.

Catching Ladybugs in Yukon

Yukon, Oklahoma, 1964

When I was five, my family shared a stockade fence with
the neighbors behind us, the Childers family—Gene
and his Chickasaw bride, LoAnne, and Gene's two sons,
Carl (who had a glass eye) and Genie (we called him
Genie with the light-brown weenie). Summer evenings
my parents would sit and drink and smoke on the patio
with Gene, who repaired cars in Oklahoma City, and his
pregnant wife from Anadarko, while I stuck bobby pins
into the outside electrical outlets, walked a couple of miles
to the creek to look for crawdads, sliced open the back of
my thigh on the sharp fender of my mother's '54 Ford,
got the wind knocked out of me from jumping too high
out of a swingset seat, and spent hours catching ladybugs
in the grass—until that night when Gene Childers poured
them out of my pickle jar onto the patio concrete and
smashed them all into mush with his fist.

Halloween

A constellation of porch lights
mirrored the stars
that small-town Oklahoma night

I cried door to door
after the older kids left
to go trick-or-treating without me.

Then Loretta Lynn and Norma Jean
warbled and whined
on the neighbors' turntable;

vodka and salt from a sip of
the salty dogs the adults mixed
stung my lips.

And later—dad passed out
across the backseat,
mother sobbing at the wheel,

the road a blur
as a storm pelted windows.
When I had to go back

and ask for the belt
my father left on her bedroom floor,
a witch cackled at the door.

Following the Red Hills Home

The Kansas guide book says turning south here is like entering another world. And it is. The land empties of people. Wind-sculpted hills rise up from the plains. At dusk, Herefords graze beneath an indigo sky. Wild turkeys roam the red canyons. Deer step out from the dark shapes of cedar trees. I've come looking for Flowerpot Mountain, a mesa made legendary by my great-great grandfather, the Pilgrim Bard, who wrote a story about a ghost named Lenora Day he saw one night spent sleepless under the stars here. He believed, as I do, that the imagined is as real as the rest of it. Now I'm chasing ghosts on lonesome roads, looking for that mythical mound. This July night there is a rare blue moon—the second moon in one month. It rises early, glows large and copper in the east. To the west: wild sky—a twilight dance of cloudscape and landscape lit by seething sun. This magical place feels more like home than any place I've ever known. The Bard's spirit haunts these hills where he wrote verse and stories more than a hundred years ago, a buffalo bone picker and poet, alone on the open prairie. But just when I see a mound shaped like an inverted flowerpot, another one comes along, then another. No cars or houses anywhere, darkness moves in, and the red-dirt road keeps circling back on itself. I realize I have no idea where I am, who I am, how to get home. I am lost in the Red Hills with only a blue moon to light my way.

Alabaster Caverns

For twenty years up north I've tried to remember what the
Oklahoma light was like. Now I'm back to see prairies
of sagebrush and mesquite, the rugged land where my
ancestors and I were born.

>After miles of cedar-dotted canyons
>and wind-blown wheatfields,
>past the steep bluffs of the Cimarron,

I stop at the area's most famous landmark. It's early
afternoon, a burning July, as I step from brutal sunshine
into dark. My teenaged guide, a farm boy from Freedom,
leads me more than half a mile underground on a private
tour of the largest gypsum cave in the world.

>We pass massive boulders of alabaster,
>all cold to the touch.
>Walls are wet, the narrow path slick.
>Seepage from the roof feeds a small stream
>that meanders through the cavern.

My guide tells me the stream was once a roaring river;
two hundred million years ago this site was covered by an
inland sea. He points out salamander and raccoon tracks
in the mud as we hike past Mirror Lake, Devil's Bathtub,
Echo Dome. The strong smell of guano is everywhere
from bats hanging high above our heads. Mid-tour in the
deep heart of the cave, he flips a switch, turns off every
light. Such dark I have never known.

>A sudden buzz of terror in the blood,
>a glimmer of premonition:
>I will know this black again.

Lights back on, my fingers find the handrail with
every step. My guide laughs when he tells me that just
yesterday his coworkers turned off all the lights, unaware
he was still in the cave. He was forced to feel his way out,
crawling on the damp floor. Now he carries a flashlight.

> We continue
> in a winding corridor
> of stone. In dim light:
> white gypsum, pink
> alabaster, pale
> crystals of selenite.

At the end of the path, at last, a wide mouth of sunlight.
Then

> meadowlark song,
> wild bursts of Indian blanket,
> cottonwoods shimmering
> against azure sky.

And I walk out dazzled into familiar brilliance, into open
arms of red earth.

Camp Houston

Midsummer and hot as hell in the farmhouse,
though the water cooler rattled its noisy air
across my grandmother's kitchen, sending
the aroma of fried chicken through all the rooms

and on out the lace-curtained windows.
Even hotter in the pickup, but we'd take any excuse
to go to Camp Houston for chocolate bars, or beef jerky,
or a bag of Fritos, while Grandad fueled the truck.

The Coca-Cola cooler waited, a gleaming red
treasure chest against the back wall. A wave of cold
met your face as you lifted the lid. Slick bottles
of Dr. Pepper, RC Cola, orange and grape soda nested

in a glistening bed of ice. God, that first swig tasted
good. So cold you wanted to hold the bottle against
your flushed cheek, then your sweating forehead.
Next to the cooler, a tall wooden box topped with glass.

A sign above it read *Baby Rattlers*. On tiptoes we cousins
peered in to see the pink and blue plastic baby rattles.
We knew the joke but had to look every time.
Twenty-five years later I bring my husband, two children,

back to see the family farm—acres of canyons
and wheat fields, barbed wire and rattlesnakes.
In the car I silently count years—twenty-two since
my grandfather was committed to the state hospital,

twenty since Grandmother's fatal heart attack,
ten that Dad has lived blind and brain-damaged by booze,

just three since my cousin was found hanging from a necktie
in his city apartment. On Highway 64, just west of Freedom,

we pass White Horse Creek, then Red Horse Creek.
From the highway I see the farm's red-dirt road rolling off
into pastureland and up and over hills like a piece
of Christmas ribbon candy. We drive on.

For miles I think it must be over this hill or the next,
until I finally spot Camp Houston, and we stop for gas.
I urge my children to come in and see the baby rattlers.
They are still there. The kids look, to humor me,

but are not amused. The woman behind the counter
is not that good-hearted-but-rough-around-the-edges one
who used to call my dad Junior when we stopped by back
then. This woman smiles weakly, says there are snakes

in a pit out back if we want to see them.
We walk behind the building, through sun-scorched weeds
crawling with red ants, to a rectangular cement pit.
That familiar dry ticking sound as we step closer.

And deep down in the dark, in heavy coils around
each other, a dozen diamondbacks hiss up at us
from shady corners, flicking their forked tongues,
rattles straight up, fangs ready to strike.

Freedom, Oklahoma Rodeo

What went on inside
the arena, I'll never know.

As moonlight rolled
across the hoods of rusty pickups
and shiny horse trailers,
my cousin Deb and I,
both thirteen, walked
the red-dirt perimeter, drinking Pepsi
from paper cups, stepping over
manure piles.

Way up in the black sky,
stars shone like pearl snaps
as we skirted stands
full of uncles and aunts, passed
vendors where pink
cotton candy sugared the air, noticing,
with sidelong gazes,
slim-hipped boys in stiff new jeans,
their rhythmic swaggering
in dusty boots.

As we made our giggling rounds,
the announcer's voice bantered
with the clowns,
and every now and then
clomping hooves drew up close behind.

At the level of our blue-shadowed eyes:
muscular thighs in leather chaps
floating past on horseback,
wheat-colored cowboy hats cocked

just right
over eyes that would almost
light on one of us,
then glance off.

All night long
our hearts waited, ready
to explode
like bulls and broncs from their chutes,

the close August air holding us
as if it would never
let go.

Tornado Warning

Around front porches
neighbors pace.
Women with arms crossed
cautiously press
bare feet to cool cement.
Their husbands
brave out
a few steps
into weed-gnarled lawns.

Chilled
by the sudden stillness,
a young mother
shoos her children
back into the house,
ready herself
to scramble
under a bed,
cheek to unswept dust.

Gray clouds loom
overhead.
Trees stand
motionless.
Telephone wires hang
expectant.

The whole town is still
as a sketch of a town
done in charcoals.

In a moment
leaves will begin to stir,
screen doors will slam.

Father's Day

O human race born to fly upward,
wherefore at a little wind dost thou so fall?
       Dante, *Purgatorio*

"Humpty Dumpty fell near here"—
the weird words I woke with
this morning, the middle of June,
Father's Day. And the last time
I talked to my dad was
a Christmas Eve phone call,
when his syllables, like the tree lights,
were vibrant, yet each flashing a separate
color, because he finally can't even
form words. Still, he tries
and tries, a string of sounds that say
nothing. And this, after losing
his sight years ago.
Drink by drink, piece by piece,
I've lost him all my life.
But I have old photos
taken when he was still
whole. In the one on my wall—
the Freedom State Bank calendar shot
from 1941—he poses
with his three little brothers:
a row of proud cowboys on the weathered slats
of the cattle-pasture gate.
Western hat, boots, a loosely-held
lariat ready at his bent, blue-jeaned knee.
Open sky and Oklahoma fields
roll out for miles behind them—
short-grass prairie ragged with mesquite,
sagebrush, sunflowers.
And I realize that the line from my dream

has something to do with
this picture, that even in sleep I cannot
rest, but must forever watch
him falling off that fence,
falling to pieces.

Grandad Scott

To this day
his name conjures a scene
I replay as if it's an old black-and-white film:
in the clearing where chickens feed
the air is still, sultry-warm.
Suddenly, out of nowhere,
an immense bird whirls down at me
from sky dark with thunderheads.
It swoops close.
Wings rasp like grain shaking into a silo.
Dirt and gravel scatter
as I run to clutch his striped overalls,
eyes aimed at his work boots.
I'm afraid to look up.
When I turn loose
there's only a far-off speck wheeling away
in sullen sky,
my grandfather roaring with laughter
because I'm a city kid afraid
of a chicken hawk.

When my brother was still a toddler,
Grandad sat him on top of his tallest tractor.
Even above the engine's deafening rumble
he could hear the two-year-old's
terrified screams. That
was Grandad's idea of fun.

That, and naming cows after
his daughters-in-law.

One afternoon
on the front porch of the farmhouse,

he told us grandkids how surprised he was
that Uncle Franklin had grown up
to be a policeman. He'd always thought Franklin
was the biggest sissy of all his four sons.

Back in 1949,
when their small town held a banquet
for my father, who was elected
national president of FFA, Grandad waited
until Grandma finished getting dressed,
then refused to go with her.
I imagine her at the bureau mirror,
silent, unclipping an earring.

Years later
he chased his youngest son Virgil
around the house,
holding a butcher knife in one hand
and a kitchen chair in the other,
lion-tamer style.
He was babbling about
Indians again, babbling fast
as a flooding creek breaking and foaming
over sharp rocks.

After that
his sons had him committed
to the state hospital. From there
it was just that Thorazine shuffle
in his baggy Big Smiths and slippers,
lips still white from windburn,
forehead still white and a shock
of white hair straight up
from decades of wearing
a stiff-billed farmer cap out in the fields.

They tell me his mother was cold-hearted.
In the flu epidemic of 1918,
his father died young.

I don't doubt Grandad lived a hard life,
trying to raise wheat and cattle
and four sons
on a Cherokee Outlet homestead
all the way through Dust Bowl days
into the era of family-farm foreclosures.

On my wall I keep a picture
so I won't remember him just as a cruel man:
in a white dress and turned-up cap,
he is a blue-eyed baby
grinning
on his daddy's lap.

Farm Wife

In the farmhouse on long
Oklahoma days
she waits
for peaches and tomatoes
to ripen, words
in her head.
Plump love-apples
line two kitchen windows
while she skins peaches.
Velvety curls drop
into a pail, pelting tin
one by one like rain
on the chicken-house roof.

Countless wedges
of angel-food cake
are cut for her husband,
neighbors when they visit,
and the sunburned strangers
who help with the wheat harvest.

Each Saturday,
wearing a dress, dark lipstick,
she drives red-dirt roads
into town to sell
her cardboard cartons
of fresh eggs.

And twice a week
she waters her multitude
of houseplants—African
violets, begonias, wandering
Jew, the tall rubber plants,

and grape ivy—while
poems lie in her
bureau drawer
and jars with handwritten labels
collect dust
in the dark fruit cellar.

FFA Jacket

My mother lifts
the dusty jacket out of her
cedar chest, hands it to me. I'm surprised
it doesn't smell of liquor: the dark-blue
corduroy jacket with the gold
Future Farmers of America emblem across
the back, his name in gold embroidery
on the left chest, and the title—
National President 1950-51.
I think of the scrapbooks full
of newspaper clippings, pictures of Dad
in this jacket at nineteen, before
college and Korea, poised
behind podiums, posing on tractors,
giving radio interviews, on TV, even tipping
his Stetson on a hometown billboard
that says *Welcome to Freedom.*
A handsome Oklahoma farm boy, the future
of America over fifty years ago. My father,
who now lives far away,
body and mind ruined by booze.
I slip the jacket on
and try to remember
for him. Mom tells me he was always
on his best behavior when
he wore it—"like Ronald Reagan
in the Oval Office," she says, "always
wore a suit and tie, out of respect, you know."
And I wish he'd never taken it off.
I'll keep it, along with his gavel,
all the eight-by-ten glossies,
and the program with the photo
of him presiding over the national convention

in Kansas City—Municipal Auditorium packed
with young men in blue jackets, some of
340,000 members that year, big brass band,
balconies draped with red-white-and-blue
banners and American flags, Dad
standing in the middle of it all,
looking, as he always has,
so utterly alone.

In the Land of Dreams

You are just one more I met along the way,
  and you are the destination.

Long days and miles have led to this voice
I hear resounding inside:
  silver crescent moon against deep black sky.

Holy daybreak, crystalline noon, lambent evening.
  Even from a distance,
  I recognized the light that surrounds you.

Now, in the calm, violet gaze of twilight,
  we find ourselves illuminated.

Circles of time have held us
  and they surround us still
  beneath rising and falling mountains,
  across rolling desert.

I am the woman with a heart of turquoise,
  eyes lit by bonfires.
Painted bears watch over my bed as I sleep.

I've traveled through a hundred twisting landscapes.
  Every trail led me here.

There were nights you nearly stopped the stars.

Find me now.
I'm never far from your window or door.
  I offer blessings lasting as stone.
  I give words to keep us warm.

Waiting for Winter Dark

Flames leap in the hearth,
the only light. Night breathes ice
onto windows. Willow branches
creak with cold.

I'm reminded again of what endures,
what returns: the flame carried
on the trail to Oklahoma
still burns.

I imagine forebears
in the Scottish Highlands, their bonfires
dancing, slate sky raining mist,
mountains a pale visage
looming on the horizon.

A glass of Glenfiddich then,
to warm the blood.

I used to think of you, love.
Now I find myself lost, searching
endless sky, alone.

Poetry is the language spoken here,
in Gaelic, in English, in Tsalagi.
Wild wind carries words
further than we could ever know.

Notes on Illustrations

Cover painting: *Family Tree* by Soleil Johnson.

Frontispiece painting: *Indian Corn* by Kathleen Johnson.

Page 5 painting: *Family Tree* by Soleil Johnson.

Page 7 photograph: The author with her mother, Marjorie Watson Cummins, and her great-grandmother, Pearl Tennyson Watson, 1962.

Page 15 photographs: The author's grandfather, A.S. Watson.

Page 19 photograph: Road in the Cimarron Breaks (also known as the Red Hills, Gypsum Hills, and Medicine Hills).

Page 21 photograph: *Ten Seconds after the Gun*, September 16, 1893, by William Seldon Prettyman.

Page 23 photograph: The author's grandmother, Minnie Sharp Cummins, with her four sons and Martha Tidwell Reed with her four sons. Freedom, Oklahoma.

Page 25 photograph: Addie May Oglevie and David Harrison Sharp, great-grandparents of the author.

Page 27 photograph: The Pilgrim Bard, Orange Scott Cummins, the author's great-great-grandfather.

Page 33 photograph: The Pilgrim Bard, Orange Scott Cummins, the author's great-great- grandfather.

Page 34 painting: *Subterranean Red II* by Soleil Johnson.

Page 39 photograph: Scott Cummins, the author's brother, and Philip Cummins, the author's cousin, in a cattle pasture on the Cummins farm near Freedom, Oklahoma, 1957.

Page 41 photograph: *Wild Ride* by Soleil Johnson.

Page 44 photograph: The author's father, Walter Scott Cummins, with his three younger brothers at the Cummins farm near Freedom, Oklahoma, about 1941.

Page 47 photograph: Oscar Scott Cummins and Walter Scott Cummins, the author's grandfather and great-grandfather, 1909.

Page 49 photograph: Minnie Sharp Cummins, the author's grandmother, on the Cummins farm near Freedom, Oklahoma, 1957.

Page 50 photograph: Walter Scott Cummins, the author's father, 1951.

Page 53 photograph: Walter Scott Cummins, the author's father, presiding over the Future Farmers of America national convention, Municipal Auditorium, Kansas City, Missouri, 1951.

Page 55 photograph: *Santa Fe Night* by Kathleen Johnson.

Page 57 photograph: *Fire* by Soleil Johnson.

Page 61 photograph: The author's great-grandfather, Orange Scott Cummins, the Pilgrim Bard.

Acknowledgments

Grateful acknowledgment is made to the editors of the following publications in which individual poems have appeared:

Wordcraft Circle of Native Writers and Storytellers, Sunday Evening Poem, September 4th, 2011: "In the Land of Dreams"

New Mexico Poetry Review: "In the Land of Dreams"

El Malpaís Review: "Three Generations of Cherokee Women: A Portrait," "The Apothecary of Minerva Best," "Ghost"

Cherokee Writers from the Flint Hills of Oklahoma: An Anthology (Cherokee Arts and Humanities Council): "Wild Sand Plums"

Platte Valley Review: "Spring Pilgrimage to Tahlequah," "Snapshots from Warr Acres," "Alabaster Caverns"

Burn by Kathleen Johnson (Woodley Press, 2008): "Frontier Bride," "FFA Jacket," "Farm Wife," "Grandad Scott," "Father's Day," "Freedom, Oklahoma Rodeo," "Tornado Warning," "Camp Houston," "To the Pilgrim Bard, in Gratitude," "Dust Bowl Diary, 1935"

Begin Again: 150 Kansas Poems (Woodley Press, 2011): "To the Pilgrim Bard, in Gratitude," "Frontier Bride," "Dust Bowl Dairy, 1935"

Cottonwood: "Dust Bowl Diary, 1935"

Kansas City Star: "Halloween"

Kansas Women Writers: "Farm Wife"

Concho River Review: "Grandad Scott," "Father's Day"

The Louisville Review: "FFA Jacket"

The Midwest Quarterly: "Farm Wife"

The Lucid Stone: "Frontier Bride"

Westview: "To the Pilgrim Bard, in Gratitude"